Not by Bread Alone

Daily Reflections for Lent 2023

908-639-1583

Susan H. Swetnam

LITURGICAL PRESS
Collegeville, Minnesota

www.litpress.org

Nihil Obstat: Rev. Robert Harren, J.C.L., *Censor Deputatus*

Imprimatur: ✠ Most Rev. Donald J. Kettler, J.C.L., D.D., Bishop of St. Cloud, May 13, 2022

Cover design by Monica Bokinskie. Cover art courtesy of Getty Images.

ISSN: 1552-8782 (print); 2692-6407 (e-book)

ISBN: 978-0-8146-6699-9   978-0-8146-6701-9 (e-book)

Introduction

"Isn't it about time for Lent again?" the woman asked. Self-identified as a "recovering Catholic," she gave a little mock shiver. "That was one of the things I hated about religion," she told me. "When I was a kid, they always pressured us to admit how bad we were. If we loved some innocent little treat, that was *exactly* what we were supposed to give up. The church looked gloomy; the homilies were stern. No religion for me! I can manufacture plenty of guilt all by myself, thank you very much!"

I'm betting that you respond to such a view of Lent with sadness, as I do. How much this woman was missing! How misguided it is to imagine this annual experience of examination, fasting, prayer, and penance as an invitation to self-loathing, when what it really invites us to embrace are life-giving new beginnings.

There's no doubt that Lent brings hard spiritual and psychological work. Frankly examining our consciences and admitting we've fallen from right relationship with God and others can inspire sorrow. Resolving to discard sinful habits and doing the necessary work of following through can challenge even the most idealistic and determined of us.

Yet there's a glorious "rest of the story" to Lent: the joyful peace that results from penance rightly undertaken. Ash Wednesday's liturgy itself echoes such peace. *Return, rise again, come back to me*, it gently invites, as readings and music recall God's ancient promise of mercy and encourage us to overcome fear and trust in loving grace. True, we can return to God anytime. But this season's Scriptures suggest with particular clarity how such reconciliation might be pursued.

The very fact that Lent comes around annually emphasizes that God's invitation is perennial. Growing in wisdom and goodness is not a matter of a one-time, one-chance, absolute conversion accomplished in a dramatic, salvific lightning flash. Instead, it's a lifelong process of second (and third, and ever-renewing) chances, one made necessarily repetitive by our sinful nature. In this spirit, Lent's familiar Scriptures and rituals invite memories of the conversions large and small that they once inspired, reminding us that despite backsliding and sin, God's arms are always open, longing to enfold us prodigals yet again.

I hope these reflections, meditations, and prayers prove a helpful supplement to the other kinds of "bread" that support you this Lent, and that your season will be one of growth, insight, and even (at the risk of astonishing those Lenten naysayers!) deeply sustaining joy.

Susan H. Swetnam

Reflections

The Lent I Skipped

Readings: Joel 2:12-18; 2 Cor 5:20–6:2; Matt 6:1-6, 16-18

Scripture:
"Spare, O Lᴏʀᴅ, your people . . ." (Joel 2:17)

Reflection: In the years immediately after my conversion, I enthusiastically embraced the practice of Lenten self-discipline, delighting in being a "real Catholic." How proud I was when all the do/don't boxes were checked off by Holy Saturday—sweets resolutely declined, time "sacrificed" to Stations, meager meals consumed, daily kindnesses accomplished. And some of those habits even stuck . . . temporarily.

Thirty years later, though, the spirit of that initial Lenten observance seems to me both childlike and wrongheaded—so mechanical, so self-satisfied, so confused about cause and effect.

The attitude adjustment began in 2002 when a loved one was dying. That year, constructing a checklist of personal sacrifices via denial of coffee or television seemed ludicrous—as did embracing *any* faith observance, then or ever again.

That was the Lent I skipped. Yet it was the one that began to teach me the difference between God's ways (mysterious, eternal-picture) and ours (transactional, short-term).

How foolish I'd been with my smug self-improvement plans, as if bean-counting success would impress a Father all-too-aware of my fundamentally sinful nature, as if I could judge and control what sacrifices were required . . . as if I could control anything.

Even vowing to undertake Lenten disciplines, our faith teaches, is *God's* inspiration, a sign that the divine is actively drawing us back. Being moved to penance is a matter for gratitude, not self-satisfaction.

These days it seems more appropriate to begin my Lents by prayerfully asking God what my particular soul requires, understanding that the actions inspired by that conversation are limited ways to address deeper needs, not currency to regain God's good will.

I've also learned to bear in mind that whatever shape renunciation takes this year, its essential goal remains the same: to address the sin that underlies all others, my ego-driven pride.

Meditation: As you make your Lenten resolutions, consider what God is calling you to do for the good of your own unique soul. Undertake your discipline in a spirit of humility, asking for the strength to persevere.

Prayer: Help me, Father, to listen for your will as I begin my Lenten journey. Let me delight in the privilege of offering my deeds and my life to you.

Daily Commitment

Readings: Deut 30:15-20; Luke 9:22-25

Scripture:
"If anyone wishes to come after me, he must deny himself and take up his cross daily and follow me." (Luke 9:23)

Reflection: My late husband, the teacher/poet/mountaineer Ford Swetnam, gave our union an immeasurable gift by insisting that the word "marriage" be considered "an active verb, not a noun." It was naive, he held, to imagine marriage as a state of stable accord achieved once and for all by a ceremony. Instead, true unions are fostered by *"being* married," as partners accept the daily work of negotiating challenges, of growing together in constant renewal of their commitment.

Today's readings imply something similar about the commitment between God and God's people. Taken as a standalone statement, Deuteronomy's message might sound noun-like and absolute, as Moses enjoins the Israelites to choose either a life of obedience or the curse of transgression. Yet its context affirms verb-like possibilities for working through difficulties. Moses' hearers have repeatedly violated their foundational contract with God, rebelliously "murmuring" on the very verge of the Promised Land (Deut 1:27). Yet

God has continually extended mercy and will do so again if the Israelites repent and reform.

Luke's Gospel also describes a human/divine bond grounded in two-way, active commitment. Both sides pledge daunting things: Jesus will lay down his life in suffering and rejection; believers will accept daily commitment to taking up personal crosses—even when doing so hurts, even when they're bored, exhausted, afraid, or doubting.

True marriage of any kind isn't easy, that's for sure. But it's exactly the kind of "active verb" relationship we're called to rekindle with God as Lent begins.

Meditation: Many couples celebrate milestone anniversaries by joyfully renewing their vows. Consider commemorating your ongoing union with God by building a small recommitment ceremony into your daily Lenten observance. Light a candle and say a brief prayer upon rising; play spiritual music or recorded rosary recitation in the car on your way to work; read the day's psalm at mid-day break.

Prayer: Help me to be a faithful and active partner in our love, O God. Teach me to see daily challenges as opportunities to build an ever-stronger foundation of commitment.

When Service Is Challenging

Readings: Isa 58:1-9a; Matt 9:14-15

Scripture:
This, rather, is the fasting that I wish:
   releasing those bound unjustly,
   untying the thongs of the yoke;
Setting free the oppressed,
   breaking every yoke . . . (Isa 58:6)

Reflection: It's hard to imagine a Christian today who would disagree with Isaiah's emphasis on charity as an essential component of a faithful life. Our pope, our Scriptures, our creed, our parish social justice initiatives, all emphasize that true worship includes serving those in need, not just following religious laws to the letter.

If you've waded into the river of ministering to the suffering, however, you've discovered that such efforts can sometimes prove unpleasant, even risky. Giving enough money to matter might require uncomfortable belt-tightening (Isaiah's listeners, for example, were financially challenged: they likely didn't consider their time of post-exile rebuilding to be the best time to liberate free slave labor). Those we serve may not always be appreciative, cooperative, or receptive. Even the grateful, gentle recipients of our care can prove emotionally exhausting despite the profound, holy joy of serving them, as any hospice worker or caregiver can testify.

Service that drains us to the point of vulnerability can feel like fasting, indeed. Yet if we're to be true to the call of Isaiah and the call of Jesus, we dig deep and carry on, abandoning the desire for immediate reward, facing down anxieties, framing the sometimes uncomfortable tasks to which we're called as sacred offerings.

Our master Jesus' service, after all, turned difficult beyond imagining. But he persisted, and that persistence changed everything for those he loved and served. So let us remember his example when service turns challenging this Lent and always, focusing not on our discomfort but on the good of those we love and serve.

Meditation: Survey your parish's website and identify which ministries seem underserved. What sacrifices might each require? What sort of risks might each involve? Ask God to help you discern whether one might be just the "fast" you need to offer this Lent.

Prayer: Give me the courage to serve you in the spirit of free and faithful sacrifice, Crucified and Risen Lord, even when I fear my efforts aren't making a difference, even when the service seems thankless.

Opening the Floodgates

Readings: Isa 58:9b-14; Luke 5:27-32

Scripture:
Then the LORD will guide you always
   and give you plenty even on the parched land. (Isa 58:11)

Reflection: As I write, the Intermountain West landscape around me is suffering from an unprecedented drought. The irrigation infrastructure that helps this high desert bloom isn't able to deliver adequate water from the mountains' thin snowpack; measurable rain hasn't fallen for months. Farmer-neighbors have had to face the tough decision to either harvest thin crops prematurely or watch their fields shrivel.

Drought comes in many forms. For Isaiah's audience the concept would have evoked both their desert homeland and the ruined Jerusalem they found as returning exiles. For us it might symbolize the desolation of illness, loneliness, or spiritual dryness—anything that feels like ongoing, hopeless barrenness.

When such figurative parching occurs, pride, shame, and our culture's insistence on self-sufficiency can discourage us from seeking essential nourishment. But consider for a moment how ridiculous those farmers would find it to refuse literal water. *That's insane!*, they'd snort. *If I could open the floodgates and let water pour in, you bet I would. There's no time for delay when you're in danger of starving.*

Thankfully, the heavenly channel of nourishing guidance always provides "plenty," as Isaiah assures us. Prayer and reconciliation can provide access to that source; so can speaking with spiritual advisors/counselors or joining a helpful, loving support group. My personal floodgates have also included wise books (notably Henry Nouwen's *Return of the Prodigal Son*) and contemplative retreats.

It's true that God will sooner or later send life-giving succor even to the most stubborn of us. But why not speed the re-blooming process, and invite the water in?

Meditation: Where do your circumstances or a loved one's seem "parched" and hopeless? Pray for the confidence to trust in God's sustenance. Look around for the sources of help that God is even now providing, and take grateful advantage of them.

Prayer: Lord of all hopefulness, help me to remember that I walk always in the shadow of your wings, even when the path seems dire. Lead me to the nourishment I need.

Accepting "No"

Readings: Gen 2:7-9; 3:1-7; Rom 5:12-19 or 5:12;
Matt 4:1-11

Scripture:
[T]hrough the obedience of the one, the many will be made
righteous. (Rom 5:19)

Reflection: Humans' tendency to push their limits—and the
often disastrous consequences—forms a perennial theme in
our stories. Innumerable tales feature protagonists who attempt to defy divine boundaries (Adam and Eve, Faust);
historical narratives and even ordinary gossip feature those
pursuing power despite warning signs (Napoleon invading
Russia; that domineering boss promoted beyond compe-
tence). When a theme has proven this compelling across the
ages, it clearly addresses a common human impulse—in this
case our species' tendency to overreaching pride.

Discerning the difference between healthy aspiration and
unhealthy "reaching" isn't always easy for us; indeed, even
deciding how far to go in petitionary prayer can be a vexing
question. On one hand, Jesus encourages bold aspiration,
inviting us to "[a]sk and it will be given" (Matt 7:7). In the
liturgy we present our intentions "with confidence"; we
routinely petition saints. Popular religious culture implies

that louder is better; just witness social media posts lobbying for "likes" to prayer requests, as if God counted ballots.

Yet you'll know from personal experience, as I do, that even our most sincere prayers, no matter how fervent and numerous, aren't always answered—or are answered in unforeseen ways. In such cases it's tempting to wonder if we haven't petitioned fervently enough, or too much.

Jesus' example certainly encourages us to pray for others' needs, and his words instruct us to lift up our own. Yet when our specific requests are categorically denied ("let this cup pass"), we must accept that a broader plan is at work ("not as I will, but as you will," Matt 26:39).

May we always trust in his wisdom, whatever response our petitions receive.

Meditation: Call to mind something you've been praying for without a clear answer or resolution, and then recall a previous similar occasion. How did God's will in that circumstance play out as time passed? Can you find peace and even surrender in your current petitionary prayer?

Prayer: All-wise Creator, grant me the grace to surrender to you when I do not get what I believe is best for me.

Our Hybrid Nature

Readings: Lev 19:1-2, 11-18; Matt 25:31-46

Scripture:
"[H]e will separate them one from another, as a shepherd separates the sheep from the goats." (Matt 25:32)

Reflection: The metaphor of good sheep versus nasty goats is such a familiar one that we are accustomed to thinking of them as irreconcilable opposites. At the risk of bucking such conventional wisdom, however, let me suggest that a hybrid species blending both sheep-like virtue and goat-like naughtiness does exist: it is called humanity.

I speak with the conviction of personal experience. Working from the criteria found in today's reading from Leviticus, I can boast some sheep credentials: welcoming strangers, comforting the afflicted, and not robbing neighbors. Honestly, though, I'm no stranger to grudges, blasphemy, or judging others.

Given that we're children of Adam and Eve, this combination of virtuous and sinful impulses seems our lot. You can probably call to mind, as I can, saintly people whose nature manifests occasional selfishness or petulance, and unpleasant people who are capable of the most charitable, kind deeds. If we believe we're held to all-or-nothing standards, we will end up discouraged or afraid.

But our God is a God of love, not fear, and today's Gospel from Matthew 25 offers us hope. Though we may be sinners, it affirms, every act of charity we exhibit is a sign that we are already receiving and sharing God's grace. First John repeats this assurance: "We love because he first loved us" (4:19). As with the desire to embrace Lenten disciplines, the good works we instinctively perform constitute signs of being loved by God and wanting to share that love with others. We may not always do it perfectly, but we keep right on trying.

Welcome to Lent, my fellow sheep with goatly tendencies!

Meditation: Reflect on occasions when you've fed, clothed, or comforted others in need. If such service felt like a natural, almost automatic thing to do, give thanks that the love of Christ is operating strongly in you, and take heart. If you undertook service more reluctantly, foster your spirit's capacity this Lent through prayer and spending time with charitable people, asking about their service and perhaps shadowing them.

Prayer: Refresh my soul with encouragement, Jesus, as I strive to fulfill the law by sharing your love.

Humble Prayer

Readings: Isa 55:10-11; Matt 6:7-15

Scripture:
"In praying, do not babble like the pagans . . ." (Matt 6:7)

Reflection: If you've ever felt uncomfortable around someone who was talking *way* too much, you probably have good instincts. Psychologists tell us that compulsive talkers are trying to dominate conversation and impose their agendas, even as their tsunami of words betrays serious anxiety.

That nugget of behavioral psychology aligns nicely with what St. Augustine has written about verbose prayer. Augustine suggests that those who engage in "much speaking" during prayer (aka "babbling") believe they can influence divine forces by "supposing that the Judge, just like men, is brought over by words to a certainty of thinking." Psychologists would nod, recognizing the attempt to overpower . . . and suggesting these "pagans" might not be quite so confident about their deities as they pretend. In contrast, Augustine notes, Jesus desires his followers to pray in relatively few words from humble yet confident "pure love," to ask while being prepared to listen. Augustine suggests that such petition, exemplified in the reverent simplicity of the Lord's Prayer, "calms and purifies our heart, and makes it more capacious for receiving the divine gifts."

Reciting the Lord's Prayer is just one of the paths toward calming receptivity that our faith offers. The Mass is full of comforting repetition. Christian tradition has developed additional ways of praying with relatively few words, including Gregorian chant and contemplative prayer. So reverently centering are these practices that scientific experiments have demonstrated their calming effect on brainwaves.

We have no need of badgering the divine in prayer. Our prayers need not consist of many words to cultivate and celebrate the abundant love that God stands ready to give us.

Meditation: Given noisy modern life, clearing the mind and heart can be difficult. If that's been a challenge for you, consider incorporating some calming form of Christian prayer into your Lenten routine. Music streaming services include Gregorian chant; websites teach Christian meditation; or simply pray the day's psalm aloud.

Prayer: God of peace, help me when I pray to rest with open heart and pliable soul, listening confidently for your voice.

Never Too Late

Readings: Jonah 3:1-10; Luke 11:29-32

Scripture:
When God saw by their actions how they turned from their evil way, he repented of the evil that he had threatened to do them; he did not carry it out. (Jonah 3:10)

Reflection: Seeing the book of Jonah listed among today's readings, we might anticipate rereading the marvelous story of the "great fish"—literally marvel-ous, as in "full of wonders." The passage we're invited to contemplate, however, focuses on "the rest of the story" after Jonah's deliverance from the belly of the fish—not as fanciful, perhaps, but a story that offers us timely reassurance for these early days of Lent.

This season's liturgy begins with such uplifting inspiration. When we're wrapped in Ash Wednesday's promise, repenting and believing seem so obviously desirable. Filled with idealistic determination, we muster our good intentions, make our vows, plan our steps.

Yet it's one thing to promise, another to deliver. It's easy enough to be good for a day or two, but habits take a long time to build or break.

We may hear ourselves saying, *Here I go again, letting God down.* I once heard the next step on that slippery slope colorfully affirmed by an old friend in a moment of self-reflection: "It's too late for me. If there's a God, I don't have a bat's chance, so I might as well do what I want."

But the story of the Ninevites shines hope into all the dark corners of our pessimism, self-doubt, and slip-ups. God takes considerable pains to send Jonah to them, after all, even bending the laws of nature! When they actually listen and respond with repentance, God is quick to relent.

So we do get a "wonder" in today's Scripture, after all, a lesson that defies our human balance-sheet mentality and our deepest insecurities: no matter how often we stumble, no matter how bad we've been, it's never too late to seek God's mercy.

Meditation: If you are already feeling discouraged this Lent, try changing your perspective. Frame this Lenten season not as a time to get everything right, but as a gift from God who longs for you. Imagine yourself among the Ninevites, making a fresh start, assured of God's love and mercy.

Prayer: Merciful God, grant me the courage to overcome my sense of unworthiness. Let me heed your call as the Ninevites heeded Jonah's, secure in your unfailing love.

March 2: Thursday of the First Week of Lent

Never Truly Orphaned

Readings: Esth C:12, 14-16, 23-25; Matt 7:7-12

Scripture:
"And now, come to help me, an orphan." (Esth C:23)

Reflection: As I write these words, a family I love is struggling with a life-changing crisis. A young couple is watching their baby, born a micro preemie at just 23 weeks, tenuously clinging to life through daily roller coasters of hope and despair. Since they've followed their son to a specialized pediatric center 150 miles away, their anxiety is compounded by separation from their three-year-old daughter, and from the home and work they love.

At the start I wondered how they could avoid sinking into despair, how they'd find the strength not to become "infant[s] crying in the night . . . with no language but a cry," as the poet Alfred, Lord Tennyson wrote when his best friend's early death shook his faith.

Yet it's already clear that God does not intend to ignore them any more than he meant to abandon Esther in today's first reading. No miracles have occurred; the baby still struggles. But many are praying for them, and grace has found numerous ways to employ such channels (even "floodgates") of divine mercy. Relatives have moved in to tend their house and foster-parent the little girl. Friends have tapped connections to arrange a house-sitting arrangement near the baby's treatment facility, providing privacy and stability. Money flows into a fundraising account. Friends send daily emails and letters to remind them that they're wrapped in love and that this is a community struggle, not an isolated, orphaned one. Their blog inspires us to tremble in solidarity with their tears and rejoice in their smiles, to dialogue, to keep praying.

Esther's story witnesses that, with God's help, no one is ever truly alone. We previously scattered friends of this couple, now one family, are learning very much the same thing right now.

Meditation: Do you feel alone or orphaned in some way? Do you know someone who does? Lift this loneliness to God in prayer, requesting comfort, trusting God will prove faithful yet again.

Prayer: Gracious Lord, make us turn to you when our lives become difficult; let us see your face in the faces of those who aid us.

Respecting Others

Readings: Ezek 18:21-28; Matt 5:20-26

Scripture:
"[W]hoever says, 'You fool,' will be liable to fiery Gehenna." (Matt 5:22)

Reflection: "I've given up on social media," my friend reports. "I got tired of hearing people insult each other. It seems like nobody takes the time to consider the other person's position or remember that a human being with feelings is reading their response."

Disrespect is the sin we seem to have forgotten is a sin, one that treats another person as less than a child of God. Contagious as a pandemic, it threatens to override all possibility of constructive, respectful relationships among diverse human beings.

Katharine Drexel's feast day is more relevant than ever in this environment, for she too inhabited an era when human dignity was besieged. Divisive thinking about "us" and "them" was widespread in those decades of the late nineteenth and early twentieth centuries. Anti-immigrant and anti-Catholic propagandists lobbied for restrictive policies and fostered violent riots. Racial discrimination against Black and Native Americans attempted to relegate a large segment of the population to second-class status.

Standing up to such hate-mongering, Drexel became an advocate for those who were openly despised by others. Born into a wealthy, high-society family in Philadelphia, she turned from a comfortable life to become a religious sister, founding a new order especially devoted to establishing educational and medical resources for those in need. Soon Drexel herself became a target. Verbal attacks and death threats came from the Ku Klux Klan. Arson menaced her schools and clinics. "Not-in-my-neighborhood" protests sparked violence. Yet Katharine Drexel, maintaining her resolute stand and modeling Christ-like dignity, never faltered in her work or sank to her adversaries' level.

Drexel's remarkable life can serve as a guiding star for us. Every person deserves our respect—in the way we speak, the words we type, and the things we do.

Meditation: Be especially aware of your interior dialogue about others today. When you catch yourself judging someone negatively, substitute empathy and offer a smile or courtesy. Pray at day's end for those with whom you interacted.

Prayer: Gracious Lord, help me to treat those I meet today as I'd treat you.

Letting Go of "Why"

Readings: Deut 26:16-19; Matt 5:43-48

Scripture:
"[F]or he . . . causes rain to fall on the just and the unjust."
(Matt 5:45)

Reflection: One bright afternoon a hospice patient's daughter stood on a porch with me, tears in her eyes. "Why did Mom have to get sick?" she mourned. "She was so vibrant, tutoring kids, planning her dream trip. She's led a healthy life. *Why?*"

There was no answer, of course, and never has been to such questions. *Why this illness? Why is this my time to die? Why do such bad things happen to such good people?*

Nevertheless, we persist in seeking answers, and sometimes the explanations we embrace for comfort are the ones that reassure us with simplistic notions of cause and effect. You'll have heard the whispers when someone is dying of a heart condition or cancer: *He brought it on himself from working too hard. She didn't try hard enough in her "battle."*

What such rationalizations ignore is that rain falls today, as it always has, on both the just and the unjust. For every Absalom who deserved what befell him, there's a Job that didn't. Sometimes we simply can't know "why."

As the possessor of a mind that loves to make sense of things, I once rebelled against that claim. But now that I work with the dying, things are different. Certainly we must ask "why" and "how" when cure and hope are possible. But experience tells me that once the end is unavoidable, there's a time for accepting things as they are. I've witnessed repeatedly how raging against the inevitable dying of the light can add emotional anguish to physical suffering, while letting go of judging what is just or unjust, and saying "Thy will be done" can inspire peace in the one who is passing that fills all who are present with faithful wonder.

And that's true in faith-challenging crises lesser than dying, too.

Meditation: Reflect on a troubling, complicated situation for which you are tempted to find a nice, neat explanation. What would be lost and gained by accepting the situation as it is, whether it can be explained or not, no matter the outcome?

Prayer: Loving Jesus, help me face the incomprehensible downpours of my life with trust in you.

Peak Experiences

Readings: Gen 12:1-4a; 2 Tim 1:8b-10; Matt 17:1-9

Scripture:
[A] bright cloud cast a shadow over them, then from the cloud came a voice . . . (Matt 17:5)

Reflection: This Sunday's Gospel acclamation ("From the shining cloud the Father's voice is heard") is among my favorites as a cantor. Having seen many shining clouds as a hiker in Idaho's mountains, I can testify to the inspirational power of skies brightened even by natural causes. Last year I stood silent and awed with friends on the eve of this "Transfiguration Sunday" on a summit gleaming with snow, valleys spread below, racing clouds billowing dark then backlit bright, as the sun edged toward setting. We weren't transfigured (except perhaps with the grace to descend safely on our cross-country skis), but the reverent wonder of that moment inflected the evening's conversation and the words I proclaimed at Mass hours later, and it still lingers in my soul.

The notion that mountaintops are conducive to spiritual insight is ancient and widespread. Lofty, wild places, it's been speculated, naturally affect our minds and emotions. Their wide views help us feel closer to heaven, their isolation banishes worldly distractions, their perspective dissolves self-absorption. "He who is not illuminated by such the great splendor of created things is blind," St. Bonaventure wrote. "Open your eyes, therefore . . . that you may see, hear, praise, and worship, glorify and honor your God."

As a people who acknowledge the synthesis between earth and heaven embodied in today's Scripture, let us raise our eyes to the heavens on this Sunday of transfiguration, and just as Bonaventure urges, let their wonder infuse our celebration with a special luminous light.

Meditation: These days the most famous naturally beautiful spots tend to be overrun with jostling crowds. Vow that at least once this Lent, you'll visit (even if virtually) a quiet, natural area with a long view (a hilltop, a broad meadow, a seashore) and spend time in silence. Allow the experience to touch, quiet, and fill your heart with awe and gratitude.

Prayer: I lift my soul to you today, Transfigured Lord, in grateful praise for the earth's inspirational beauty, the sky's uplifting glory.

Repenting Together

Readings: Dan 9:4b-10; Luke 6:36-38

Scripture:
"[W]e have rebelled and departed from your commandments . . ." (Dan 9:5)

Reflection: What power a simple pronoun can have! "[W]e have rebelled," Daniel says. Instead of exhorting others with "you" or using an equally self-distancing "they" as some prophets do, the peerless Daniel—interpreter of dreams, conduit for God's word, community spokesperson, tamer of lions—grammatically lumps himself among the transgressors.

All who serve God are bound to acknowledge that sin is part of human nature, including their own. But publicly admitting to personal faults, as Daniel does here, is a very different matter.

I was once among those halfway folks who went to private confession but shrank from community reconciliation services. Believing that my occupation and my liturgical duties made others expect a higher standard, I imagined them thinking, *The teacher and writer has feet of clay! Who is she to instruct others?* Or in the case of those who knew me well, *I hope she's going to confess x, y, and z!*

Finally, though, one year's schedule left me no choice but a Lenten penance service. What a revelation! What sympathy and reverence! That night I felt for the first time that I was a true member of my faith community—seen, known, accepted among equally vulnerable brothers and sisters with no need to pretend, one among many who were mutually relying on grace. I count that night as my actual conversion.

I'll bet that Daniel would also be a fan of community penance services if he lived today, given his willingness to stand among sinners. Let his example give us courage, imagining his voice raised with ours this Lent as we intone, *Be merciful, O Lord, for we have sinned.*

Meditation: If you've always celebrated private confession, try attending a community penance service this year. Put aside any fear or embarrassment, remembering that others have also humbled themselves. Let the communal air of sorrow and hope wash over you, renewing your membership in God's family.

Prayer: Lord, melt our pride and help us draw strength from one another as we turn to you in repentance.

March 7: Tuesday of the Second Week of Lent

The Freedom of Discipline

Readings: Isa 1:10, 16-20; Matt 23:1-12

Scripture:
Come now, let us set things right,
   says the LORD . . . (Isa 1:18)

Reflection: Among the happiest weeks of my year is the one I spend on retreat at a Benedictine monastery. It's hard to imagine a friendlier, more creative, or more fulfilled group of women than these religious sisters. So it seems odd to hear them pitied. "That lifestyle is so regimented," someone opined on learning of my visits. "Losing your freedom to think for yourself and do what you want when you want would be awful."

"Discipline" and "orderly life" might seem like stodgy concepts these days. Yet that monastery radiates not oppression but a peaceful freedom from the chaos so typical in secular life—the demand overload, the chaotic interruption, the anxiety and burnout. Governed by St. Benedict's Rule, its days are orderly. Shared housework has its hours, as does labor at individual callings; prayer, mealtimes, socializing, and free periods come around regularly. These sisters rise every morning knowing there will be time for everything that matters, every day. No wonder they're serene.

Inspired by convent life, I've incorporated what structure I can into my own noisy, necessarily varied days, setting aside daily meditation time at rising, striving for regular meal and sleep hours, holding myself to a regular writing time, walking outdoors after lunch, completing chores in the afternoon. Though I'm by nature an anxious, speedy person, even this modest regimentation is yielding happy results. I wake with a relaxed, expansive sense of the day, feeling at least a taste of convent serenity infusing my spirit and body, approaching my work with better, holier focus.

Urging those who "hate discipline" (Ps 50:17) to "set things right" (Isa 1:18) isn't a divine effort to crush our will. It's a call to break certain kinds of chains and be free.

Meditation: Do your days feel harried and scattered? Try incorporating one or two non-negotiable scheduled intervals into your day or week for things God would want you to do. Consider refreshing leisure as well as important work.

Prayer: Help me to order my days, Lord, so that I may grow in the freedom to serve you.

Humble, Hidden Service

Readings: Jer 18:18-20; Matt 20:17-28

Scripture:
"[W]hoever wishes to be great among you shall be your servant . . ." (Matt 20:26)

Reflection: "I'm getting my COVID shot tomorrow!" an elderly hospice patient's spouse exalted. "Not here in town," she added. "They don't have any more. That sweet Dr. Brooke is driving three of us 'oldsters' all the way to American Falls. She got reservations for us!"

Dr. Brooke is an esteemed, influential physician, a pioneering local gerontologist. She's been retired for three years. These are her *former* patients. And she's a member of our parish, by the grace of God.

While every form of charity Christians offer in God's name surely makes the heavens sing, such humble, hidden deeds as Dr. Brooke's—compensated only by the satisfaction of helping others in need—must raise a particularly enthusiastic angelic chorus. Driving for half an hour each way, reassuring anyone who is anxious, listening patiently to stories she's certainly heard before, will never show up on any published roster of donations, won't draw new patients even if she were taking them, and won't garner public admiration. But the difference she's made by serving others in this modest way is extraordinary, assuring these good folks that some-body sees them, somebody cares.

As someone who's been on the receiving end of this kind of care lately, I can speak to its power. Recently an anony-mous neighbor has started bringing my empty trash can back up the driveway on Mondays—a long, steep, often icy challenge in this late winter season. On that day my work schedule stretches into early evening and I return to a dark, empty house. What a wonderful sense of being wrapped in community that simple gesture provides! And how much better I sleep on Monday nights knowing I've been "seen" and cared for.

And how deeply it reminds me that extending modest, everyday grace to others just might be the most profound way of all to honor our servant-leader Christ.

Meditation: Review the acts of service you've offered these first few weeks of Lent. Consider which were hidden from public view. Vow to prioritize such private acts of charity between now and Easter.

Prayer: Redeem and purify my soul, humble Christ, so that I may serve with your humility.

Seeing Others' Pain

Readings: Jer 17:5-10; Luke 16:19-31

Scripture:
He is like a tree planted beside the waters . . . (Jer 17:8)

Reflection: Before we can serve others as true stewards of God, we must be willing and able to see their needs. Pope Francis has suggested that such "seeing" involves not just eyes but feelings, urging us to "open the doors of our hearts to others," in contrast to the Gospel's rich man, for whom Lazarus was practically invisible.

Ironically, the fragile nature of our hearts can tempt us to turn aside from others' pain. Many of us feel an instinctive unease when faced with suffering, as with a baby's crying. Such things remind us of our vulnerability to physical hunger, lonely abandonment, illness, and death. Primal fear whispers that such a fate might be transferrable, urging us to flee.

The response is often different, however, in those who have survived their own hard times. Once you've been hungry or lost, it's hard to turn away from those who are suffering, whether indications are obvious, as in someone who lives on the streets, or more subtle, as in someone who is struggling with internal anguish. Sympathy and empathy just naturally well up.

Such survivors make especially effective ministers. Among those I know are a high school teacher who attempted suicide in her teens and now gently, persistently reaches out, saving lives; social workers who minister from lessons taught by their own troubled birth families; and a hospice chaplain who offers companionable, comforting balm hard-won from losing both of her parents.

"Make us your bread, broken for others," proclaims a hymn appropriate for both the Easter Vigil and Ordinary Time. If you sing it in your church, bear in mind that some sitting nearby might feel a shiver of recognition in these words. Ask God to bless them with the grace to continue seeing. And if you've been so seasoned, include yourself.

Meditation: Has life broken you? What did that breaking teach you about vulnerability, suffering, sharing, and healing? How do you, or how might you, put that awareness into action, bearing fruit to nurture others in their seasons of need?

Prayer: Crucified Christ, let us follow you in serving others until all are fed.

Contending with Envy

Readings: Gen 37:3-4, 12-13a, 17b-28a; Matt 21:33-43, 45-46

Scripture:
When his brothers saw that their father loved him best of all his sons, they hated him . . . (Gen 37:4)

Reflection: Envy presents a unique challenge among human sins because its causes, psychologists say, are rooted in deep-seated insecurity beyond our conscious awareness. Its age-old contagion has been documented in innumerable dark legends. Seeing someone else preferred, as Joseph's brothers did, can still spark fears that there won't be enough resources or love to go around.

Envy is so ingrained in our nature that it manifests even in "innocent" life stages, as demonstrated by the first graders in my Brownie troop shoving each other aside to grab the pink crayons. It's deliberately promoted in adult contexts, both professional (bosses pitting subordinates against each other for promotions) and recreational (winners getting prizes and accolades while "losers" look on).

How corrosive the resulting self-doubt, ruthless competition, and fears of abandonment are! How they divide us from each other!

Yet there's one realm in which envy need not trouble us at all, thank heavens (literally): our yearning for the heavenly

Father's love, the most important need of all. As a chorus of wise Christian voices reminds us, divine favor is wide enough to encompass everyone. Hildegard of Bingen joyfully proclaims that "God's loving maternal embrace" is extended to all. And Pope Benedict XVI reassures us, "Each of us is the result of a thought of God. Each of us is willed, each of us is loved, each of us is necessary."

This Lent, let us remember that glorious truth, turning from insecurity, relaxing into that embrace.

Meditation: The next time envy threatens you, call to mind someone so secure in God's love that he or she wholeheartedly celebrates others' successes. Take a deep breath, remembering that God holds you, too, in the divine heart, and ask for a generous spirit.

Prayer: All-embracing Creator, may the awareness that your love is never rationed give me strength to resist that old enemy, envy, and live peacefully with my brothers and sisters.

Indwelling Hope

Readings: Mic 7:14-15, 18-20; Luke 15:1-3, 11-32

Scripture:
Who is there like you . . .
Who does not persist in anger forever,
   but delights rather in clemency . . .? (Mic 7:18)

Reflection: I often catch myself wondering how the Prodigal Son could have mustered up the courage to return home, much less have the *hutzpah* to hope for even a minimal welcome or employment. How likely was it, really, that his father would employ such a miscreant? Given his situation, I certainly would have faltered, anticipating rejection, coldness, a sibling's disdain—hope-killers, all.

Yet return he did, as do the prodigal sons and daughters among us who embrace improbable hope every day. They beg pardon for fracturing relationships; they regroup after rebellion or failure and return to family, occupation, faith. And all of us who turn our Lenten steps toward God must count ourselves among their number.

"Hope is the thing with feathers - /That perches in the soul - /And sings the tune without the words - /And never stops - at all - ," Emily Dickinson wrote, celebrating our innate capacity to pick ourselves up and dust ourselves off, trusting in the possibility of rebirth. Plenty of actual tunes testify to an indwelling capacity for optimism in our species. From Gustav Mahler's *Second Symphony*, to the old hymn "Softly and Tenderly," to the Bob Marley ballad "Redemption Song," such music inspires us with promises of unity regained. Micah's words in today's first reading constitute a sixth-century-BCE version of such a song, using pastoral imagery to feed the listener's longing for the Shepherd's care.

How wise our Lord is to have endowed us with the hopeful capacity to pursue—even against odds of our own making—exactly what he wants us to seek!

Meditation: Pray in thanksgiving for "the thing with feathers," the holy hope that inspires you to seek clemency this Lent, that makes the very idea of forgiveness seem possible. Consider seeking out sacred music that evokes confident hope in divine mercy and download it as a soundtrack for your season.

Prayer: Let us praise the God who makes all hope possible.

Mundane Routine/Transformative Encounter

Readings: Exod 17:3-7; Rom 5:1-2, 5-8; John 4:5-42 or 4:5-15, 19b-26, 39a, 40-42

Scripture:
"Is the Lord in our midst or not?" (Exod 17:7)

Reflection: You've undoubtedly heard homilies offering the typical interpretation of Jesus' encounter with the woman at the well: it's an emblem of Christ's outreach to sinners. The well's water stands for the living water of salvation; when the woman accepts Jesus' truth and evangelizes, she models right Christian action.

So obviously accurate and authoritative does that interpretation seem that I found myself temporarily stymied at writing this reflection. How could I avoid just repeating what you already know?

Yet God provides, I'll attest in awe, for yesterday inspiration found me during an impossibly busy day. I was running late for appointments; the car's gas indicator glowed red; the only available pump was half-blocked by a carelessly parked minivan. I muttered unrepeatable words. I even grudged the beloved hospice work ahead. Then the offending driver called over: "Dr. Swetnam?! I'm sure you don't remember me, but you were my professor. You inspired me to become a teacher!" She rushed to hug me.

Suddenly the afternoon's ministry looked more like privilege than tedious, time-consuming labor. Perhaps I'd touch another life today.

Afterwards I came home to write from a new sense of common ground with that long-ago Samaritan woman, who had also experienced a revelatory encounter during a harried, mundane routine. Drawing water would have been a boring chore for her, a tiresome, necessary part of daily life, like pumping gas was for me. She would have had many obligations waiting. Others at the well wouldn't have been always perfectly behaved—especially to her. Yet it was there and then that her transformative meeting with Christ occurred.

Let us remember that God can choose to touch our souls at any moment, reaching into the tedium of our days when we least expect it, changing everything.

Meditation: Regular routines can harden our hearts and close our ears and eyes in boredom, resentment, daydreaming. The next time you catch yourself not fully present in a "mundane" moment, resolve to look for the gifts God might be offering.

Prayer: Help me, O Lord, to live my days ever-awake to the possibility of meeting you at any turning of the road.

From Exceptionalism to Humility

Readings: 2 Kgs 5:1-15ab; Luke 4:24-30

Scripture:
"[I]f the prophet had told you to do something extraordinary, would you not have done it?" (2 Kgs 5:13)

Reflection: "My back is much better after doing the stretches you showed me," my dietician friend and sometimes massage client says. I congratulate her, observing that she's the exception—most ignore such strategies, assuming that steroid shots or exotic vibrating gadgets will be more effective on "my level of pain."

"I can relate," she smiles. "Getting healthier is so basic for most people: eat less, move more, avoid excess sugar and fat. But many want complicated fad diets and expensive meal plans. As one of my patients put it: 'I'm not "most people"!'"

Self-proclaimed exceptionalism also manifests in the spiritual life. "It's funny," a priest friend observed. "I've seen people disappointed when their only penance is repeating the Lord's Prayer. Their faces say, *That's ALL, Father? How can that be enough?* They seem invested in thinking they're exceptional sinners."

Naaman's story testifies that such a sense of "specialness" is not a modern invention. No doubt this wealthy, powerful man directed a look at Elisha that said: *That's ALL?* He was expecting a scene worthy of his status: a dramatic laying-on-of-hands with gasping spectators, a head-turning public sacrifice. But he was simply told to take a bath—in a dirty, provincial river.

Fortunately for him, Naaman was persuadable, and that modest baptism of sorts both cured and converted him. Or as St. Augustine—who considered humility the foundation of all other virtues—might suggest, perhaps Naaman was cured not by the washing itself, but by his *willingness to submit* to this mundane act, as if he were just like anyone else.

May we remember Naaman's story whenever we imagine that ordinary measures—in faith and in life—aren't sufficient for our special selves.

Meditation: After Naaman's bath, he becomes "like . . . a little child," an image evoking smallness and dependency (2 Kgs 5:14). How do you need to be reborn into humility this Lent? What small acts of obedience can contribute?

Prayer: God of the humble, allow me, like Naaman, to do the simple things you ask.

Top-Down Forgiveness

Readings: Dan 3:25, 34-43; Matt 18:21-35

Scripture:
"[D]eal with us in your kindness and great mercy. Deliver us by your wonders . . ." (Dan 3:42)

Reflection: As a Protestant adolescent and an accountant's daughter, I was always intimidated when we prayed, "Forgive us our debts, as we forgive our debtors." I understood all-too-well that one column in my account with God—forgiveness— stood hopelessly in the red. The issue wasn't my intentions—as an almost too-good girl, I struggled to extend mercy to the bullies who made my life miserable. But I just couldn't, and the shame of my failure only compounded my everyday anxiety.

The resulting sense of cosmic injustice—*Bullied and damned? No thank you!*—helped to fuel my college break from religion. Two decades later, though, after an innate yearning that I couldn't ignore led me into the catechumenate, the truth about forgiveness became clear.

"It is not in our power not to feel or to forget an offense," I read one afternoon. In wonder and relief, I finally heard the reassurance our church offers. Being unable to forgive on my own wasn't confirmation of my own faulty character, but was simply the reality of my human situation, a manifestation of the general flaw of original sin. When we suffer a wrong, when bitterness troubles our souls, the only way to break the cycle is to turn to God, asking honestly for the grace to forgive.

The prayer of Azariah in today's first reading or the cry of the psalmist to "Create in me a clean heart, O God" (see Ps 51:12) are beautiful expressions of this dynamic between ourselves and God. Mercy isn't something we conjure from some heroic capacity within ourselves; it's a gift available for the asking, flowing down from God's infinite supply.

Meditation: Saints who forgave their persecutors just before death demonstrate God's ability to bless us with the ability to forgive even in extreme circumstances. Investigate the life of such a martyr, perhaps St. Stephen, St. Maximillian Kolbe, or Blessed Leonella Sgorbati, a Consolata Missionary Sister murdered in 2006 as she left the Somalian teaching hospital she'd founded, whose last words were "I forgive, I forgive, I forgive." Meditate on the person's relationship with God. Pray for the gift of forgiveness toward someone who's wronged you.

Prayer: Infinitely forgiving Jesus, open my heart with your mercy; make me merciful.

March 15: Wednesday of the Third Week of Lent

Teaching by Example

Readings: Deut 4:1, 5-9; Matt 5:17-19

Scripture:
"But whoever obeys and teaches these commandments will be called greatest in the Kingdom of heaven." (Matt 5:19)

Reflection: Clare, one of my hospice patients, is in her late eighties. Once an active woman, the owner of a successful needlework store, a world traveler, and a lifelong learner with a rich social life, she's now confined to an assisted living facility and is facing serious health problems. Yet her days are among the most inspirational I've ever seen, a testimony to how sustained faith and love can enlighten even life's most difficult periods with meaning.

Adapting her routine to the mandates of evolving circumstances, devout Catholic Clare worships online via her tablet, "going" to daily Mass and checking out parish religious education presentations. She serves others by making friends with her caregivers; indeed, she's become a quasi-grandmother to the young CNAs, who share their troubles and ask her advice. She prays with uplifting music; she welcomes priests and visiting ministers. She retains her lively interest in God's created world, surfing websites featuring natural wonders and diverse cultures; she cultivates a garden of potted succulents. To share her peaceful, accepting presence is a delight, a lesson in God-inflected aging that encourages more hope, less fear about growing older.

If you're a professional educator as I've been, what probably comes to mind when you hear the injunction to teach, as in today's Gospel, is a dedicated instructional setting, complete with well-defined goals, lesson plans, and specialized pedagogy. Clare's example, however, stands as a vivid reminder that every one of us is a teacher all the time. Even in situations some would consider almost unbearable, it's possible to demonstrate the most essential lesson of all: life is always better for those who trust in God.

Meditation: Do you know anyone whose demeanor and actions suggest a life lived in the promised land of faith? Before Lent ends, make a point to spend time with that person, learning, growing, and absorbing his or her spirit.

Prayer: May I grow in faith, O Lord, so that my life may radiate your goodness to all who witness it.

Balancing Speech and Silence

Readings: Jer 7:23-28; Luke 11:14-23

Scripture:
Jesus was driving out a demon that was mute, and when the demon had gone out, the mute man spoke and the crowds were amazed. (Luke 11:14)

Reflection: The "demon that was mute" in Luke's Gospel is definitely an odd biblical specimen. Demons in Scripture are characteristically nasty blabbermouths who inspire disruptive, impious words from their hosts.

In our world, too, "noisy" often means negative. Impassioned online posts deafen us with polarized rants; shouting media voices model antagonistic conversation habits. Excepting soundproof rooms or country retreats, a cacophony of voices, honking horns, humming machines, and blaring tunes challenge sustained thought and prayerful awareness. No wonder anxiety and sleep deprivation are widespread problems.

Luke's silent demon, though, reminds us that sound—even loud sound—isn't always a bad thing. Imposed silence can be a curse for citizens of repressive regimes; unspoken truth can sully families, workplaces, and society. I'll wager that in your case as in mine, for every cringe-inducing memory of something you regret saying, there's an equally painful memory of something left unsaid.

In the book of Ecclesiastes, we read that there is "an appointed time for everything . . . a time to be silent, and a time to speak" (3:1, 7). But how can we know what's best in a moment's heat? Perhaps we can ask ourselves what best serves God's will in that moment. After all, it's the Lord who has appointed the "timeliness" of everything, speech and silence included. Speech that sustains another person, that invites understanding, that effects charity, that celebrates what's good is called for. Words that do the opposite aren't.

Let us be vigilant, then, in listening for God's voice as we strive against demons both loud and mute, seeking to discern timely from untimely speech, merciful silence from cowardly.

Meditation: Have you spoken too much or too little in an important situation lately? If so, vow to pay attention the next time you're tempted to one extreme or the other, praying to understand how love may best be served.

Prayer: May your will always inform the messages I offer, Lord, whether articulated aloud or manifested in silence.

March 17: Friday of the Third Week of Lent

Dreaming of the Garden

Readings: Hos 14:2-10; Mark 12:28-34

Scripture:
Again they shall dwell in his shade
    and raise grain;
They shall blossom like the vine . . . (Hos 14:8)

Reflection: What a beautiful picture Hosea paints of a lush garden landscape, complete with dewy lilies and fruitful, shady olive trees! When I was a lector and proclaimed this passage, I fancied I could see the congregation's shoulders relaxing, eyes softening, smiles appearing.

And how timely its encouragement is for this mid-point in Lent, when honest examination may reveal much left to do in the way of fulfilling Ash Wednesday's earnest intentions. Just as we might be running out of steam, drifting, or discouraged, our liturgy in its wisdom touches our hearts and imaginations as well as our minds and consciences.

The effect goes deeper than pretty pictures and gentle cadences, of course. Researchers in landscape studies argue that gardens are tonics for our spirits, automatically encouraging a sense of secure happiness (unless, perhaps, the backyard badly needs weeding!). Studies have documented that people physically relax when contemplating open green spaces ringed with blooming plants, perhaps because our instincts recall the human race's savannah origins and feel, *I'm home.* Scripture's account of human origins in Eden adds a sacred component to the nostalgia.

It's no wonder, then, that Hosea's imagery of trees, vines, and flowers provides a practically irresistible metaphor for the rewards of serving God. May it open our spirits today, touching that ancient comfort, cheering us as we continue on our Lenten road.

Meditation: Do you have favorite Bible passages that read like poetry, using imagery, metaphor, and rhythm to move emotions? Make them a regular part of your reflections. Keep your ear tuned at Mass and in daily devotions, noting those that "speak" to you, and browse in Psalms and Song of Songs for new favorites.

Prayer: Loving God, open my ears to hear your voice through the beauty you've created, both in words and in the gardens of this world.

Real-Life Renewal

Readings: Hos 6:1-6; Luke 18:9-14

Scripture:
"[The LORD] will heal us;
  . . . he will bind our wounds.
He will revive us after two days;
  on the third day he will raise us up,
  to live in his presence." (Hos 6:1-2)

Reflection: I once met a man who, on learning that I am Catholic, proudly described himself as a "very tolerant atheist." But the good impression for which he was striving evaporated with his next remark: "Hey, if religion helps you sleep at night, I'm all for it!"

The prophecy of Hosea in today's first reading might seem to such a person a perfect example of a pie-in-the-sky fairy-tale designed to soothe the anxious minds of pathetically insecure believers. For us active believers, however, it reflects a very real situation, one already playing out in the here-and-now through extraordinary real-life renewals. I recall a young mother escaping an abusive husband, whose parish members bound her wounds and participated in her revival, helping her remake her home and move forward in security. I have seen the joy of an immigrant family adopted by a local church, for whom a modest way of life without threat of violence is experienced as healing and wholeness. I remember a teenager born with an apparently fatal physical condition who by God's grace now anticipates a full round of normal life.

Hosea's assurances are not the stuff of fantasy. They are an expression of an ongoing relationship, one tendered by a God whose fidelity is already beyond dispute. This God doesn't patronize us with fairytales; as the very one who's given us rational minds, God is more than willing to provide concrete signs of healing and binding, of his presence here and now, that help us sleep secure in peace.

Meditation: What evidence of God's healing and renewal have you experienced or observed? When have events caused your doubts and fears to be replaced by confident faith? Have you been privileged to already experience a "revival" in some aspect of this life through God's goodness? Share your stories, listen to others', and give thanks together.

Prayer: Loving God, when I despair, help me to remember the many times you have already healed and revived me.

Keeping the Circuit Open

Readings: 1 Sam 16:1b, 6-7, 10-13a; Eph 5:8-14; John 9:1-41 or 9:1, 6-9, 13-17, 34-38

Scripture:
Live as children of light, for light produces every kind of goodness . . . (Eph 5:8-9)

Reflection: All the "children of light" I know—and I know many—radiate holy, joyful energy. So unfailingly strong is their bright kindness that you might fancy it comes as electricity does, through a direct line from the source of all love.

Such connection with the "holy power grid" is even more striking when contrasted with those who decline to connect. You've undoubtedly met some of them, people like an acquaintance of mine whose engagement with life was so weak that contact with her drained even my normally bodacious energy.

There was nothing objectively wrong with this woman; she possessed health, abundant means, and an attentive, loving daughter she'd recently moved to join. Yet she found our town as unattractive as the place she'd gladly left. "There's nothing to do here!" she grumbled bitterly. I suggested she seek friends and activity at church. *Not religious.* How about volunteering to tutor reading, or joining the friendly circle making blankets for nursing homes? *Not inter-*

ested. Subscribing to the town's continuing education group to share an interest or learn something new? *Too much trouble.* Soon she moved again.

Hers was among the saddest lives I could imagine. Yet more than once its memory has saved me when my own mind has whispered, *Too much trouble.*

Having known her confirms what those children of light demonstrate: opting into the ever-flowing "electricity" of God, becoming a conduit of that light and power, illuminates not just the lives of others but our own.

Meditation: Call to mind an "illuminated" person you know, someone whose company inspires love, security, and holy vigor. Close your eyes and remember the details of what it's like to be with him or her—how do presence, gestures, words speak of God's indwelling? Ask God to renew a glowing spark of divine energy in you, and cultivate those outward signs of inward connection.

Prayer: Ever-radiant God, spark my life with your light. Help me to brighten and refresh the souls of all I meet.

March 20: Saint Joseph,
Spouse of the Blessed Virgin Mary

Fostering

Readings: 2 Sam 7:4-5a, 12-14a, 16; Rom 4:13, 16-18, 22; Matt 1:16, 18-21, 24a or Luke 2:41-51a

Scripture:
I have made you father of many nations. (Rom 4:17)

Reflection: As a childless woman in a region where families run large, I've often cringed at the default conversation-opener—*"How many children do you have?"*—anticipating the awkward silence and wounding pity my reply often triggers.

These days, though, I happily proclaim the operational truth. "A daughter," I say, picturing Shelley, once my graduate student, now as close as any biological child could be. Every few days we talk across a 150-mile separation; we regularly meet for writing retreats and hiking weekends; she's sous-chef for my ridiculously large Christmas party. Her husband and teenager are tolerant, indeed.

Or I say, "Two daughters," including Lara, a beloved former girl scout who's "inherited" my enthusiasm for complicated baking and travel to far-flung places.

The truest answer might actually be hundreds, if you include the students who've followed my path into teaching and stay in contact. To have been a teacher for forty years, it appears, is to become the Old Woman Who Lived in a Shoe.

Raising biological children is a magnificent calling. But parenting others' biological children—whether in an adoptive or foster setting, or as a blood relation (aunts and uncles, grandparents), or as a mentor provided by life's circumstances or God's hand—is not a consolation prize. It's a calling with its own joys and responsibilities, challenges and triumphs, holy in its own right.

Consider, after all, that St. Joseph himself is simultaneously the patron of fathers *and* foster parents. St. Joseph, pray for us!

Meditation: On this feast day, recall mentors who have touched you in life-giving ways. Thank God for them, and, if they're living, contact them to express gratitude. Thank God also for those you've mentored or are mentoring, and consider honoring St. Joseph by reaching out to someone else, young or old, who could use your loving support. You might even consider asking a lonely elder to mentor *you*—a priceless gift for you both.

Prayer: Remembering St. Joseph, O Father God, I lift my voice in gratitude for the gift of parenting in all its forms.

The Blessing of Water

Readings: Ezek 47:1-9, 12; John 5:1-16

Scripture:
Wherever the river flows, every sort of living creature that can multiply shall live . . . (Ezek 47:9)

Reflection: As I was making dinner, a gentle, insistent rain began spotting the skylight. As noted earlier, moisture has been especially scarce lately in the region where I live. This month has set an all-time regional drought record, and ten days have passed without the merest shower. Lilac bloom is three weeks late; the Forest Service has diverted a creek beside a favorite mountain trail to flow through a pipe instead of dancing down its natural course. "The volume's so low, it's not going to reach the lower meadow on its own this year," a ranger explained when we met on the trail.

The sound of raindrops quieted my breathing, relaxed my heart. And I noticed that another creature had registered the change: my old orange cat, who had clambered atop the sofa by the big window and was gazing, rapt and meditative, across the valley at the soft clouds drifting over mountain ridges.

Ezekiel makes water a metaphor—an emblem of God's grace, a sign of the blessings of paradise and eternal life—another lovely example of Scripture's textual richness.

That rainstorm, so intrinsically moving that it entranced a cat, reinforced not just rain's literary quality but it's absolute literal wonder as a fragile gift not to be taken for granted.

Pope Francis has reminded us that we're stewards of God's creation, called to "ecological conversion," called to be people who more wisely shepherd the earth's resources. Pollution and exploitative carelessness that disrupt regular weather behavior, he's warned, represent a betrayal of that holy trust.

As today's readings stir us by evoking heavenly abundance, may they also inspire us to renewed stewardship of the finite blessings our planet holds.

Meditation: We all tend to take the earth's resources for granted. Think of one way you can turn carelessness into good stewardship—reducing waste or energy consumption, or using less water, for example. Offer this act of care for creation as part of your Lenten practice, and consider continuing it into the Easter season and beyond.

Prayer: Gracious God, help me do my part in keeping our earth a viable home for "every sort of living creature" (Ezek 47:9).

Miracles 1: Invited to Dream

Readings: Isa 49:8-15; John 5:17-30

Scripture:
"For the Father loves the Son and shows him everything that he himself does, and he will show him greater works than these, so that you may be amazed." (John 5:20)

Reflection: "Be realistic" is generally good advice. Yet it's temptingly easy to cross the line between reasonable ambitions and much-too-optimistic dreams—especially given the contemporary notion that anyone can achieve anything with sufficient positive thinking. A student expects top grades for minimal effort; a beginner undertakes a project beyond his skills; me the time I seriously injured myself by adopting a training goal absurdly beyond my fitness level.

Today's readings remind us that the terms "realistic" and "unrealistic" aren't working categories for God, however, or for what we can expect from God's hand. Isaiah enumerates wonders: the dead raised, prisoners freed at a word, mountains leveled, barren plateaus made pasture-like and safe from heat and wind. Though framed thousands of years ago, these images retain their power, especially for those who minister to the incarcerated, travel outdoors in high rough country, or lose someone dear.

But perhaps such dreams are not so "wonder-ous" after all. Although miracles might seem improbable or incredible to us, they seem quite natural to God. "Unrealistic" lies in the eyes of the beholder.

In that spirit let us take courage in this season of seeking God, daring to entertain our outrageously aspirational longings to see God's face, daring to trust in heavenly ways nothing like our own.

Meditation: A friend of mine has coined the term "Lenten fatigue" to express the sense of flatness that can occur as these forty days progress, despite all good intentions and dedication. Are you feeling that way? Refresh your soul by noticing examples of God's extraordinary in-reaching as you go about your day. What figurative raisings, liberations, and leveling of difficulties do you observe? Let this practice energize your fatigue as we move into the final weeks of Lent.

Prayer: When my steps falter, marvelous God, bear me up with just the miracles I need.

March 23: Thursday of the Fourth Week of Lent

Accepting God's Guidance

Readings: Exod 32:7-14; John 5:31-47

Scripture:
"I see how stiff-necked this people is." (Exod 32:9)

Reflection: "Stiff-necked" had a very specific association for the ancient Israelites, referencing oxen who would not obey the plowman's direction, beasts so stubborn they ignored the goads employed to control their speed and guide them in straight furrows. Since life depended on agriculture, such headstrong animals (with their giant appetites) were worse than useless, and those who persisted in disobedience would soon find themselves discarded, or dinner.

Oxen aren't alone, of course. The animal kingdom is full of strong-willed creatures. Numerous sayings acknowledge this—we speak of the tendency of sheep to wander, the impossibility of "herding" cats, the stubbornness of mules. And numerous biblical passages use these metaphors to describe human behavior. Isaiah 53:6, for example, compares us to sheep, with our tendency to go "our own way."

Headstrong as oxen and wandering like sheep? Sounds pretty human.

Yet God offers guidance for our headstrong, wandering ways. Scripture directs us. Friends and family advise us. The Spirit whispers to us through our consciences. We may be as headstrong as ever, and we may sometimes strain against taking a new direction, but there is hope for even the most "stiff-necked" among us!

As Lent continues to unfold and we acknowledge our disobedience and our wandering ways, let us also remember all the psalms and stories that remind us how slow to anger our God has been through the ages, how warmly God welcomes penitents back, how patiently God guides the oxen and pastors the sheep.

Meditation: Is there an area of your life where you are constantly bumping into obstacles, leading you to suspect that you may be going in the wrong direction? Might these be touches from the divine plowman's guiding rod? How might these experiences be leading you to change course? What new direction might you take?

Prayer: Teach me your ways and let me accept your guidance, God, even when I think I know best.

Righteous Unsettling

Readings: Wis 2:1a, 12-22; John 7:1-2, 10, 25-30

Scripture:
"To us he is the censure of our thoughts;
 merely to see him is a hardship for us . . ." (Wis 2:14)

Reflection: While Hollywood tends to cast young actors in the roles of heroic priests, the man I heard challenging his congregation several years ago had retained his fervor for social justice well into middle age. As a traveler I knew no one in that church, yet my co-worshippers' unease was clear in their tight faces, squirming, and murmurs. Whatever the reason they'd come to Mass, it wasn't to be challenged to address social injustices.

He's not long for this parish, I thought with a sad smile, reflecting that at least he wasn't preaching in a time and place where such a bold message might court physical danger.

But Óscar Romero did. This saint, whose feast day is today, made it his business to shake the status quo in his homeland of El Salvador. Preaching against an iron-fisted, dictatorial realm that "disappeared" the poor and opponents, he made enemies of both civil and religious establishments. His fearless proclamation of justice ultimately led to his martyrdom.

"A church that doesn't provoke any crises, a gospel that doesn't unsettle, a word of God that doesn't get under anyone's skin, a word of God that doesn't touch the real sin of the society in which it is being proclaimed, what gospel is that?" Romero asked.

May we not be quick to dismiss those whose words challenge us; may we remember that Jesus Christ himself made people extremely uncomfortable.

Meditation: Few of us have the courage or eloquence of Óscar Romero, but we can find ways to honor his legacy of speaking truth to power. The next time you encounter a contemporary prophet whose advocacy for justice ruffles feathers, listen with an open heart, imagine one modest thing you can do to apply that message, and do it.

Prayer: God of justice, send holy ones to challenge my complacency. Help me to hear them, and let my courage grow in the light of their example.

Saying "Yes"

Readings: Isa 7:10-14; 8:10; Heb 10:4-10; Luke 1:26-38

Scripture:
". . . I am the handmaid of the Lord. May it be done to me according to your word." (Luke 1:38)

Reflection: As Catholics we think of the word "annunciation" with a capital "A," as in the glorious feast we celebrate today. Yet annunciations appear in everyday lives, too, in the sense of moments when the future changes radically, irrevocably, in a moment.

Those "lower-case annunciations" might be joyful or they might be unwelcome—a child is conceived; we discover a new calling or are ousted from a comfortable one; a loved one dies; a disaster, illness, or financial windfall touches us. What these annunciations share is the sense of disruption they spark, the dissolution of who we thought we were, the imperative to rethink who we might become.

When such abrupt change strikes us, Mary's response to the angel Gabriel—though beyond any surrender we might be able to imagine ourselves making—offers a model of life-sustaining acceptance. The Gospel story depicts Mary's initial response as the kind of healthy human questioning any reasonable person might raise. Described as "greatly troubled," she asks: "How can this be . . . ?" Some Renaissance artists even paint her as shrinking back, pale and over-whelmed, as in Fra Angelico's famous "Annunciation." (If you're struggling with denial regarding change, praying with such images might comfort you, as they did me.)

Artists' renderings aside, Scripture clearly indicates that Mary does quickly commit herself to God's direction, affirming her willingness to accept whatever comes, offering a model of how even the most drastically blindsided of us might follow suit.

Let us remember her when we're abruptly called to something that we may not understand. Let us persevere through disruption and anxiety; let us learn to say yes.

Meditation: If you're struggling with what appears to be a call from God for a serious change in your future, spend time focusing on Mary's story, on images of her, and on the mysteries of the rosary. Let her example strengthen and inspire you.

Prayer: Loving God, help me navigate the watershed moments of my life with trust in your plan for me.

Miracles 2: Do You Hear Me Now?

Readings: Ezek 37:12-14; Rom 8:8-11; John 11:1-45 or 11:3-7, 17, 20-27, 33b-45

Scripture:
Then you shall know that I am the LORD, when I open your graves and have you rise from them, O my people! (Ezek 37:13)

Reflection: Jesus' miracles strengthen our faith in numerous ways. They demonstrate his unity with God; they teach us as living parables; they invite us to marvel at divine power.

Even their sequence of intensity is instructive, demonstrating just how brilliantly God works with our skeptical nature, attracting us and easing us into belief with smaller miracles, then dazzling us with great. Turning water into wine is a wondrous thing, no doubt, one that speaks to our yearning for earthly plenty. Healing peoples' illnesses moves us by touching our desire for health in ourselves and those we love.

But raising people from the dead? That kind of miracle touches our deepest possible despair and might well be difficult to believe if we hadn't been "warmed up." And even within this category of miracles, incidents are arranged in ascending order of wonder, as St. Augustine observed. Jesus' first such miracle involves a young girl so recently deceased that she's still in her bed (some might claim she was simply comatose); the second a dead young man removed from his home but not yet buried (stranger things have happened than delayed revival). But today we hear of a man four days dead, buried, and presumably decomposing, so there's absolutely no chance that he hasn't in fact died. Nobody could imagine that his rebirth wasn't miraculous.

Jesus' own resurrection brings the pattern home with culminating effect, preparing for the ultimate miracle of the resurrection of all believers.

How could any attentive listener dare to scoff at such evidence? How can we not hear God now?

Meditation: Have past occasions inspired doubt in you about God's power? What aspects of your life have tempted you to question? Review Jesus' miracles, and meditate on one that speaks with particular power to your current circumstances. Pray for open ears and stronger faith.

Prayer: Risen Christ, may we affirm "Yes, Lord" as Mary of Bethany and Mary of Nazareth did, whenever skepticism whispers.

Advocacy for the Vulnerable

Readings: Dan 13:1-9, 15-17, 19-30, 33-62 or 13:41c-62; John 8:1-11

Scripture:
The whole assembly cried aloud,
blessing God who saves those who hope in him. (Dan 13:60)

Reflection: Though the two women in today's readings both face condemnation, their differences are striking. Susanna is virtuous; she lives in wealth and has supportive relatives; she's being framed for a sin she didn't commit. The woman depicted in John's Gospel, in contrast, has indisputably sinned and appears abandoned by all her friends; she stands alone with her judges. Nevertheless, both women are equally vulnerable—they stand accused with little recourse of their own.

These readings invite us to contemplate how we might advocate for the vulnerable among us. They also draw us to think about our own position before that absolute judge, God. Most of us, as sinners all-too-aware that condemnation would be appropriate, will resemble the second woman much more than we do Susanna. Though friends may support us on earth, their testimony won't go far in that heavenly court; neither will our wealth nor status.

How fortunate we are that our ultimate judge is not a rigid, earthly authority, but the God who said "Neither do I condemn you" and who inspired Daniel to trap Susanna's accusers in their contradictory lies.

How glorious it is that this very judge is eager to lighten the burden of sin we'll ultimately bring before him!

Meditation: Over whom do you have earthly power in your family, at work, or in other situations? The next time you're faced with a "sentencing," imagine what Jesus might say as advocate for the other person, and what *you* might say if you were appointed their advocate. Consider those insights as you make your decision.

Prayer: Guide me in right paths as I'm called to correct others, O God, and deal mercifully with me when I face judgment.

Facing Up to Transgressions

Readings: Num 21:4-9; John 8:21-30

Scripture:
"Make a saraph and mount it on a pole, and whoever looks at it after being bitten will live." (Num 21:8)

Reflection: "One thing you can say about God in the Old Testament—he's *very* interactive," my friend says. I smile, having been myself long fascinated by these colorful stories of God's involvement with human beings, featuring big personality, candid one-on-one conversations, and dramatic manipulations of natural phenomena.

This bold and mysterious way of God is on full display in today's first reading. Why would God ask the Israelites to make a bronze saraph (snake or serpent) and approach it for healing from the bites of the very serpents that God inflicted on them as punishment for idolatry?

Much interpretive ink has been spilled on this weird story, as you might imagine. One explanation highlights snakes' revered healing power in ancient medicine and analyzes this event as another example of God's merciful relenting. Other interpretations identify the statue as an allegory for Christ's cross—Christians look upon his suffering to be healed, just as the Israelites looked upon this strange object.

At the risk of presuming, let me suggest that this story also anticipates a truism of modern counseling: acknowledging a problem is essential to its healing. That bronze snake doesn't only symbolize Christ's suffering; it embodies the precise cause of the people's own. Just as an alcoholic in a twelve-step program is encouraged to admit dependency, those idolators are compelled to look their idolatry literally in the face, to acknowledge their transgression and consequent pain.

It is much the same for us, you might say, in the sacrament of reconciliation, as we "hold up" our sins—admitting and acknowledging them—before we can be pardoned.

Maybe that story isn't so weird, after all.

Meditation: Have you participated in the sacrament of reconciliation this Lent? If not, face the saraphs/sins in your own life. Yes, it may be uncomfortable ("saraph" means "fiery," as in burning venom). Take courage, though, in knowing that God has established this sacrament precisely because he wants you to come home, to be fully healed.

Prayer: O Lord, let my cry come to you. Let me not continue in denial of my sin.

March 29: Wednesday of the Fifth Week of Lent

Real Truth, Real Freedom

Readings: Dan 3:14-20, 91-92, 95; John 8:31-42

Scripture:
"[A]nd you will know the truth, and the truth will set you free." (John 8:32)

Reflection: Jesus' remark that "the truth will set you free" is surely among the most widely applied—and misapplied—of all his sayings. As a 1960s teenager I knew it as a rallying cry for social/political protest: *Speak/act up boldly and become liberated from society's lies!* People still quote it to justify too-frank confrontations in relationships. Secular universities use it as a motto championing worldly knowledge. It's even carved in stone (literally) on the original CIA headquarters.

Challenging ignorance and the status quo can certainly be good, scripturally approved things. Yet it's clear from John's account that Jesus meant something else. Freedom from *sin* is what true freedom means, Jesus says ("everyone who commits sin is a slave of sin"; 8:34), contradicting his hearers' association of the term with social liberation ("We . . . have never been enslaved to anyone"; 8:33).

Jesus' kind of freedom isn't a quick or happy ticket to self-actualization or power in this world. Indeed, many who follow him will suffer as he did even unto death, as martyrs still do; some who hear the call to conversion will remain slaves, as slavery still exists in many forms.

Instead, as Father Richard Rohr has written, Jesus' freedom paradoxically demands surrender. When we let go of "what traps us . . . our small self, our cultural biases, even our fear of loss and death" and agree to trust God absolutely, we're liberated from the constant anxiety of such preoccupations, from the hopeless responsibility of managing our own destiny.

What a counterintuitive kind of freedom this is! No wonder so many have misunderstood.

Yet, as people seeking to live as God's children, it's the freedom to which we're called.

Meditation: Rohr notes that many things can keep us enslaved, including grasping for power, security, esteem, and material possessions. Where is your fearful need so strong that you are resistant to allowing Christ to set you free? Allow yourself to feel that craving, then prayerfully imagine relinquishing it into Christ's loving arms.

Prayer: Help me find freedom, Lamb of God, in surrender to the Father.

March 30: Thursday of the Fifth Week of Lent

Marking a New Direction

Readings: Gen 17:3-9; John 8:51-59

Scripture:
"No longer shall you be called Abram; your name shall be Abraham . . ." (Gen 17:5)

Reflection: One of the things I like best about being a member of our parish's Easter Vigil music group is the physical proximity to candidates and catechumens as they're received into the church. It's especially moving to stand nearby as they are called by the names of the saints they have selected for patrons, watching faces glow with the joy of having become someone new, affiliated with an admired holy one. It's poignant to ponder what backstory or aspiration might have inspired these choices—Padre Pio, Mary Magdalene, Maximillian Kolbe, Catherine of Siena, Dymphna. When a woman selected my patron, Elizabeth Ann Seton, I spontaneously hugged her after Mass, awash in empathy and fellow-feeling for a presumptive kindred spirit.

Choosing a new name or having one chosen for you, as in Abraham's case, has for eons been a sign of new identity, something associated with transformation and a new phase of life. Abraham's new name is certainly prophetic of upcoming events: it means "father of multitudes" as opposed to just "noble father."

Names give us something to live up to; they keep us on track. Whether we embrace a new version of an old name (the young adult shift from "Susie" to "Susan" was revolutionary in my case), a patron saint's name, or a title to which we aspire—"Patient Mother," "Advocate for the Homeless," "Ethical and Fair Judge"—identifying ourselves in a new way can help us become different, better people.

What are you calling yourself these days?

Meditation: Are you close to a patron saint? If so, offer prayerful thanks and do something in his or her honor during Holy Week. If not, research saints to find one whose circumstances echo yours or who models how you aspire to live. Ask for daily guidance, and in your own mind, dare to call yourself by that saint's name.

Prayer: Help me to discern the name you've chosen for me, O Lord. Let it shape me as you desire.

Talking Frankly to God

Readings: Jer 20:10-13; John 10:31-42

Scripture:
O Lord of hosts, you who test the just . . .
Let me witness the vengeance you take on them. (Jer 20:12)

Reflection: Jeremiah is certainly frank in conversing with God—so familiar his tone might seem almost inappropriate. He asks directly for what he desires, although in some cases it is decidedly harsh (*Let me see them suffer!*). He expresses wry anger, accusing God of duping him as one might betray an intimate friend (20:7). What a contrast to the formal, generic way we tend to pray!

Nevertheless Jeremiah's relationship with God is one to be envied, a model of intimacy. Perhaps we might consider borrowing a page from his book, granting that as in marriage or friendship being straight with each other—even clearing the air occasionally—is essential for healthy alignment.

I proclaim this, admittedly, as someone whose relationship with God became perversely more distant after my beloved husband's death. Like a sullen spouse in a failing marriage, I spun internal, self-serving narratives regarding grievances rather than opening dialogue with God. Especially in regard to the question that seemed most urgent—*Why wasn't I being granted the death I prayed for?*—I convinced myself that this greedy God wouldn't let me go until I'd completed some-thing-or-other still pending in his service.

A hail of worthy deeds ensued—darts thrown vigorously at an unknown target. *Let's get this over with!*

Nothing worked, but eventually stubborn reserve broke—or was helped to break. One night, still very much alive, I placed myself in a classical posture of heavenly address out on the deck, hands open to the stars. "Is that sufficient?" I heard myself ask aggressively, aloud. "Will you beam me up now, for heaven's sake?!" Abruptly I was laughing at the audacity—and that moment began the rest of the story.

"I went a little crazy that night," I admitted later to my spiritual advisor.

She smiled. "Oh, no. I think you were starting to go sane."

Meditation: Are you in the habit of sharing your thoughts and feelings frankly with God? If the idea seems frighteningly forward, review accounts of plain dealing by Moses (Exod 4:10-17), David (Ps 13), or Jeremiah (Jer 20:7-13), and remember that openness builds intimacy. Start a conversation.

Prayer: Guide me in revealing myself to you, Father, so that our relationship might deepen.

April 1: Saturday of the Fifth Week of Lent

Sensing What's Coming

Readings: Ezek 37:21-28; John 11:45-56

Scripture:
[H]e prophesied that Jesus was going to die for the nation
. . . (John 11:51)

Reflection: While we may find ourselves saying, "My good-ness, it's Holy Week already!", the daily readings have of-fered signs of Christ's impending crucifixion, accumulating and intensifying ominously with each passing day. Initially came murmurs and skepticism from Jesus' contemporaries, then nit-picking persecution ("You shouldn't heal on the Sabbath!"). In yesterday's Gospel, Jesus narrowly escaped being stoned; today the plan to execute him is affirmed.

If you've ever floated a whitewater river, the sense of looming confrontation might call to mind places where a canyon's narrowing and steepening speeds the water's flow, where a muted roar signals turbulence around the bend.

Those visiting Jerusalem for Passover didn't fail to notice those signs, assuming Jesus would flee trouble. Yet after just a brief breath-catching retreat, he returned boldly, accepting and even sealing his fate.

I wonder if Jesus mused as his passion loomed that his three years of ministry had been far too short, as we might reflect when a noteworthy interval in our lives closes, or if he told himself that the pain would last only a little while, as we might before surgery. Whatever his thoughts, he walked willingly, one foot in front of the other, to the cross.

The story of that reckoning, Lent's culmination and core, lies immediately before us on this eve of Holy Week. As diligent Catholics we will steel ourselves to follow its flow in the reading of painful words and the fulfillment of solemn obligations, feeling the river spill over the initial ledge, riding a turbulence that threatens to shake faith.

It won't be comfortable, and others might skip this part of the ride.

But it's the least we can do.

Meditation: How do you respond when you sense an inevitable crisis coming? Do you try to ignore it, hoping it will disappear? Or do you pray and face it boldly, trusting God? Meditate on Jesus' incredible courage through the days ahead.

Prayer: Mighty God, keep me ever in your care when looming troubles daunt me.

April 2: Palm Sunday of the Passion of the Lord

The Here and Now

Readings: Matt 21:1-11; Isa 50:4-7; Phil 2:6-11; Matt 26:14–27:66 or 27:11-54

Scripture:
[O]thers cut branches from the trees and strewed them on the road. (Matt 21:8)

Reflection: My friends and I grinned as we emerged from the cathedral in Prague one Palm Sunday a decade ago, delighted by the budding pussy willow branches we'd been given in keeping with regional tradition to wave for the procession. How charming and earth-friendly it was, we told each other, to choose a locally abundant, free sign of new life for this celebration!

Exploring the central marketplace, the famous sites, the ordinary neighborhoods that day, we kept noticing others fresh from church with pussy willow branches tucked under their arms or peeking out of their purses.

Palms would have made the commemoration of Jesus' entry more historically accurate, sure, but somehow those humble branches made it more vividly immediate. *If Christ had entered Prague today versus Jerusalem centuries ago*, those pussy willows suggested, *this is what would have been abundant enough to gather and wave. And look how festively glorious this familiar little spring budding is!*

There's no doubt that historically accurate reenactments of biblical events can inform and inspire us—whether through expensively produced films or parking lot creche scenes with living animals. Yet there's much to be said, too, for remembering that we Christians aren't just pretending to be some long-distant crowd.

For God's blessings still manifest as everyday, local beauty in our here and now. And the love of our Savior still calls us, on days triumphal *and* ordinary, to use any happy thing that comes into our hands in celebration of his glory.

Meditation: What seasonal foliage might you wave if Jesus entered your town today? Are azaleas or forsythia blooming? Are shrubs just starting to green up? Bring such local evidence of rebirth into your prayer space as a symbol of Lenten new beginnings. Pray for the grace to continue saying "Hosanna in the highest!" long after the immediate excitement of Holy Week and Easter Sunday have passed.

Prayer: King of Glory, let me remember that my own acclamations, promises, faithfulness, and betrayals of you matter as much as those recounted in Scripture.

Seize the Day

Readings: Isa 42:1-7; John 12:1-11

Scripture:
"You always have the poor with you, but you do not always have me." (John 12:8)

Reflection: One of my friends, a respected engineer, admits that his dream was always to be a professional photographer. As a talented adolescent, his images impressed teachers and won state fair sweepstakes (best-of-best) ribbons. The pressure to study something practical was too intense to resist, however, and photography is now only a hobby. "Maybe when I retire, I can get serious again," he says. "But sometimes I do think about where I might be if I'd gone for it."

Surveys studying "quality of life" reveal that opportunities postponed and lost haunt many of us. "Go on the trip; spend the time with loved ones; reach for your dreams," advise those who passed up such opportunities, paraphrasing counsel given centuries ago by the Roman poet Horace, who urged readers to "seize the day."

Today's Gospel tells of Mary of Bethany seizing one of her days, a profoundly timely moment, to pour out oil and love during her family's last dinner with Jesus. What a comfort that memory would have been even a week later—though

Jesus had suffered, at least he died knowing how they honored and treasured him.

How tragic it is when chronic prudence becomes extended procrastination! What a bitter food irredeemable regrets can make!

"Work, for the night is coming," Anna Coghill's nineteenth-century hymn with that title advises, a message relevant to many things, including pursuing vocation, building relationships, and practicing faith.

How might your Holy Week observances be different if you knew this year would be your last?

Meditation: Remembering Mary of Bethany, ask yourself if there are people who would benefit from (or who long for) demonstration of your love and admiration. Reach out to them during Holy Week. Don't wait for a more convenient time.

Prayer: Creator God, grant me the energy and openness to embrace each day's opportunities.

April 4: Tuesday of Holy Week

The Reassurance of Being Known

Readings: Isa 49:1-6; John 13:21-23, 36-38

Scripture:
Reclining at table with his disciples, Jesus was deeply troubled . . . (John 13:21)

Reflection: Outsiders to our faith might wonder how we can believe in a God-man who shows vulnerability, who could be "deeply troubled" at a mere mortal friend's betrayal, who asks his father that a cup of pain might pass, who feels physical anguish and emotional abandonment on a cross. Shouldn't a deity be above suffering, sublimely un-anxious and detached from earthly troubles? How can anyone rely on a supernatural being so . . . human?

How surprised such a person might be to learn that the answer, according to St. Ignatius of Antioch (among others), is that we can rely on Christ *precisely because* he reflects features of our human experience that might seem "un-god-like" in some conceptions of divinity. Disputing the early Christian heresy of Docetism (which held that Christ's body was just an apparition), Ignatius argued that Jesus' physical body sets an unassailable precedent: a being who suffers and dies—just as we do—can have eternal life.

We can also find reassurances in Christ's behavior on this earth. Take, for example, the tendency to worry. If you find yourself often anxious in the watches of the night, as I do, you might be inclined to judge your faith inadequate. If we really believe, shouldn't we be able to proclaim, "In peace I will lie down and fall asleep" (Ps 4:9)?

Holy Week's events remind us, though, that we follow a Savior who also stayed awake in mental turmoil while others slept, a redeemer who experienced dread, who is described as feeling anxious and troubled (Mark 14:33-37; John 12:27). Wise in the ways of our imperfect nature, he's in the position to offer perfect empathy and utterly reliable guidance through all of our falterings.

Let us rest peacefully in his arms, in the comfort of being fully known.

Meditation: The next time you find yourself lying awake, troubled with doubts and worries, turn to a comforting, repetitive prayer like the rosary. Imagine the Shepherd sitting at your bedside, wishing you peace.

Prayer: May I remember your suffering when my own comes, loving Jesus, and seek you confidently, knowing you understand.

Good Trouble

Readings: Isa 50:4-9a; Matt 26:14-25

Scripture:
The Lord God is my help,
    therefore I am not disgraced . . . (Isa 50:7)

Reflection: The late civil rights leader John Lewis spoke of getting in "good trouble," the persecution that often results from challenging an immoral status quo. This concept of suffering for righteousness' sake echoes through our readings as the Triduum nears: Isaiah recounts how preaching God's truth has brought violence and shaming; the psalmist documents insults; the story of Judas's betrayal anticipates Christ's suffering.

While preaching the truths of faith can still get a person killed in many countries, fortunately this price is rarely paid in America. Yet our brothers and sisters here frequently encounter opposition—and violence—for advocating principles aligned with Christ's teachings.

Some of these, like Lewis, become national icons, but less conspicuous examples turn up in just about any town or institution. You probably know such bravely outspoken people: the woman on the city council who keeps developers honest when desire for profit threatens the poor or the environment; the colleague who advocates for students' or patients' or clients' good above fiscal expediency. You'll have witnessed the insults and shaming—perhaps expressed through stony silence or eye-rolling, perhaps by punitive consequences—that still threaten those who rock the boat.

If you're among those courageous ones, God bless you. If you're more reticent about getting into good trouble, consider how you can support the prophets in your midst when their persecution comes, instead of drawing back to safety.

How can we walk the next three days in good faith with Jesus, after all, if we're simultaneously betraying his heirs?

Meditation: No matter what your creed, gender, national background, or profession, it's likely that in the past someone has risked standing up to authority on your behalf. Research one of these honored mothers/fathers—whether a family member, social activist, or saint—and light candles for them during the Easter season. Write a note of appreciation to a living advocate of righteousness.

Prayer: God of Justice, may I always be "firm, steadfast, always fully devoted to the work of the Lord," even when troubling consequences might result (1 Cor 15:58).

Following Jesus' Path of Sacrifice

Readings: Exod 12:1-8, 11-14; 1 Cor 11:23-26; John 13:1-15

Scripture:
"I have given you a model to follow, so that as I have done for you, you should also do." (John 13:15)

Reflection: From its earliest years Catholic tradition has revered martyrs. We honor their homelands with pilgrimages and their death dates with feasts; our art depicts them wearing golden crowns. Early Christian tradition held that suffering death as faithful witnesses earned immediate unity with the martyred Christ in heaven.

Acclaiming martyrs, however, is quite different than imitating them. While we stand in awe of the bravery of martyrs both historical and recent, their terrible fates represent a trial that all but the best of us, I'm pretty certain, would prefer to skip.

Yet according to Pope Francis there's hope for us, too, to wear at least a version of a martyr's "starry crown" (in the words of the old gospel song). In an address honoring contemporary martyr Óscar Romero, Francis explained that "giving life does not only mean being assassinated" but can also entail, in Romero's own words, "giving life a little at a time . . . in the honest fulfillment of one's duty; in this silence of everyday life." Every small sacrifice we voluntarily offer in the spirit of love testifies to our solidarity with Christ. Every instance of "dying" to some personal desire by putting others first qualifies: when a poorly-paid career in service is chosen over worldly riches, when free time is sacrificed for a child's enrichment, when we wash the feet of another person in any number of ways.

Such offerings might seem pitifully dim reflections of Jesus', Sebastian's, or Romero's glory. Yet these sacrifices, too, reflect the path of losing our lives in order to find them, as modeled by Christ (Matt 16:24-25).

Let us then perform our "little martyrdoms" with eager joy, understanding that they, too, light the way to glory.

Meditation: As you commemorate Jesus' sacrifice during this Triduum, notice the everyday self-denials in your life and the lives of those around you. Take heart, understanding that these small sacrifices reflect and build your relationship with Christ.

Prayer: Crucified Christ, may I bear witness to your power in the willing ways I "lose my life" a little at a time.

Seeking God in Silence

Readings: Isa 52:13–53:12; Heb 4:14-16; 5:7-9; John 18:1–19:42

Scripture:
[B]ecause of him kings shall stand speechless;
for those who have not been told shall see,
   those who have not heard shall ponder it. (Isa 52:15)

Reflection: Today we commemorate what must have been a disruptively cacophonous episode with deep silence. John describes chaotic action: the ear cut off, Jesus seized, the soldiers' insults, the crowd's shouts. Those crucified would have groaned and screamed; their friends would have wailed.

Nevertheless, we believers remember that day in reverently still churches. We go forth mute at our services' end, not allowing conversation to break the profound tenor of what we've just experienced. Each soul is left alone to contemplate the sorrowful mysteries.

How countercultural this is in our hyper-communicative twenty-first century! Conventional wisdom urges us to talk through unsettling events with others, to seek advice that explains and manages them. "Brooding" too much in silence is considered unhealthy.

Centuries of people seeking to feel closer to God would beg to differ, however. Following Jesus' example, monastics, mystics, and believers everywhere have regularly immersed themselves in silent, solitary reflection, believing, as Sr. Joan Chittister has written, that only in silence does God speak to the heart.

Few of us can keep Good Friday with an all-day contemplative retreat, given work and family responsibilities. Do your best, though, to experience a taste of reverent listening at the day's services, embracing this timeliest of invitations to open your mind and spirit to truths too profound for words.

Meditation: In addition to devotional reading and public worship, consider making time this evening or tomorrow morning for a mini-retreat. Find a quiet place where you can be alone and reread today's readings. Resist overthinking; just sit with the great mystery of Jesus' suffering and death, asking God to let it touch your heart and soul.

Prayer: Speak to my heart, O Crucified Christ, as I contemplate your infinite love for me. Let the awed silence in which I sit become a hymn of praise to you.

This Most Sacred Night

Readings: Gen 1:1–2:2 or 1:1, 26-31a; Gen 22:1-18 or 22:1-2, 9a, 10-13, 15-18; Exod 14:15–15:1; Isa 54:5-14; Isa 55:1-11; Bar 3:9-15, 32–4:4; Ezek 36:16-17a, 18-28; Rom 6:3-11; Matt 28:1-10

Scripture:
You will show me the path to life,
   fullness of joys in your presence,
   the delights at your right hand forever. (Ps 16:11)

Reflection: Though any anniversary or annual celebration invites memories and stock-taking, the Easter Vigil uniquely inspires us to recall both our collective and individual faith histories. What a scope of time its readings recount, drawing us back through the millennia to demonstrate God's covenant faithfulness. What reassurances it offers: that earthly pain is only temporary; that Christ's sacrifice will bring redemptive, loving union; that mourners will be comforted and faults forgiven; that "festivities of unending splendor" await us when this earthly life ends, as proclaimed at the lighting of the Easter candle.

Surely it's a rare mortal who isn't moved by these promises. And for those who struggle and despair on this holiest of nights, they'll ring with an even greater, more immediate, and personal charge.

If you've ever been a member of that tribe, you may find all future Vigils glowing with a particular light. You may shiver, like me, on hearing phrases in the Easter Proclamation that once seemed written just for you, and remember how joining this night's communion procession once felt like an incredible privilege rather than a routine thing. You might give thanks that grace has led you to a time of relative peace, and pray for those among the assembly who struggle this year, asking that they too might be comforted and strengthened in the faith as Easter dawns.

How beautifully this once-a-year celebration of praise and promise culminates our Lenten sacrifices! What a life-affirming, ever-beckoning "path to life" our God opens before us—on this night and always.

Meditation: As you read through the Vigil readings or participate in the Vigil Mass tonight, note which celebratory moments, Scriptures, songs, or phrases especially touch you. How do they reflect what you need to hear this year? Consider gathering with others during the early days of the Easter season to share your insights. If possible, plan to attend the Easter Vigil next year and invite someone new to accompany you.

Prayer: Ever-faithful God, may the sanctifying power of this night fill my heart with comfort and gladness.

April 9: Easter Sunday: The Resurrection of the Lord

Celebrating Renewal

Readings: Acts 10:34a, 37-43; Col 3:1-4 or 1 Cor 5:6b-8; John 20:1-9 or Matt 28:1-10

Scripture:
This is the day the LORD has made;
　let us be glad and rejoice in it. (Ps 118:24)

Reflection: Even though the Vigil Mass keeps me up *way* past my bedtime, my custom for decades has been to greet Easter morning early, eagerly rising for an annual, intentional sacrifice of walking praise.

As the sun crests the mountain ridges in the national forest near my home, I'm usually swathed in a warm jacket and woolly hat. It's still early spring at 5000' elevation in Idaho, and sometimes this ritual occurs in falling snow. The forest road is paved, but the surrounding country is wild—its juniper-covered ridges rising steeply, its canyons dense with vegetation. The creek rushes with snowmelt; deer, beaver, mink, and the occasional moose come to drink; hawks soar. Late Easters are graced by the earliest spring flowers— glacier lilies, fritillaries, spring beauties.

Though an electronic soundtrack enlivens my typical daily walks, I leave the iPod at home on Easter mornings, when the music of the spheres and reflections on the resurrection seem vastly more appropriate. I review the Lenten season, thanking God for the grace to have been faithful in at least some respects, vowing to persist where I've stumbled. I savor insights and joys offered by the season's liturgy. I set intentions for the Easter season unfolding before me and pray that new ways of witnessing to God's love might emerge.

Simultaneously, though, I take care to be present in this sacred slice of God's earth. Noticing is appreciating, after all, and there's so much to inspire gratitude here, so many signs of the year's faithful turn.

Thank you, Lord, my soul sings, *for earth's blossoming and ever-renewing life.*

Meditation: What signs of God's faithful renewal do you see on this Easter Day? How has your life been refreshed with new hope? Invite those with whom you gather today to share their own observations, and rejoice together.

Prayer: Risen Jesus, may this Easter Day's spirit of joy live on in my heart through all the year's turnings.

References

February 28: Tuesday of the First Week of Lent
St. Augustine of Hippo, *Our Lord's Sermon on the Mount*, Book 2
  (12–16).

March 2: Thursday of the First Week of Lent
Alfred, Lord Tennyson, "In Memoriam A.H.H." (1850).

March 5: Second Sunday of Lent
St. Bonaventure, *The Journey of the Mind to God* (15:1), http://
  web.sbu.edu/theology/bychkov/itinerarium_oleg.pdf.

March 9: Thursday of the Second Week of Lent
Pope Francis, Message for Lent, 2017, https://www.vatican.va
  /content/francesco/en/messages/lent/documents/papa
  -francesco_20161018_messaggio-quaresima2017.html.
Bernadette Farrell, "Christ, Be Our Light" (Oregon Catholic
  Press, 1993, 2000).

March 10: Friday of the Second Week of Lent
Hildegard of Bingen, "The Trinity," from *Scivias*, Part II, Vision
  2. *Hildegard of Bingen, Selected Writings* (New York: Penguin
  Classics, 2001), 21–22.
Pope Benedict XVI, Homily at St. Peter's Square, April 24, 2005,
  https://www.vatican.va/content/benedict-xvi/en/homilies
  /2005/documents/hf_ben-xvi_hom_20050424_inizio
  -pontificato.html.

March 13: Monday of the Third Week of Lent
St. Augustine of Hippo, Letter 118, Chap. 3 (22).

March 14: Tuesday of the Third Week of Lent
Catechism of the Catholic Church, 2nd ed. (United States Catholic Conference—Libreria Editrice Vaticana, 1997), 2840–2841.

March 17: Friday of the Third Week of Lent
The "savannah hypothesis" was proposed as early as the 19th century by J.B. Lamark and Charles Darwin, among others. For a discussion of the effect of park-like landscape on humans, see Jo Barton and Mike Rogerson's "The importance of greenspace for mental health," *BJPsychInt*, Nov. 2017; 14 (4): 77–81, https://www.ncbi.nlm.nih.gov/pmc/articles/PMC5663018.

March 21: Tuesday of the Fourth Week of Lent
Pope Francis, *Laudato Si'*, On Care for Our Common Home (2015), 220, https://www.vatican.va/content/francesco/en/encyclicals/documents/papa-francesco_20150524_enciclica-laudato-si.html.

March 24: Friday of the Fourth Week of Lent
Óscar Romero, Radio Sermon, Feb. 18, 1979. Collected in *The Violence of Love*, trans. James R. Brockman (Maryknoll, NY: Orbis Books, 2004). For an account of Romero's life, see also Kevin Clarke, *Oscar Romero: Love Must Win Out* (Collegeville, MN: Liturgical Press, 2014).

March 25: The Annunciation of the Lord
This entry references the fresco in the north dormitory hall at the Church of San Marco in Florence, but many of Fra Angelico's other depictions of the scene also suggest that Mary was initially unsettled.

March 26: Fifth Sunday of Lent
Catechism of the Catholic Church, 2nd ed. (United States Catholic Conference—Libreria Editrice Vaticana, 1997), 547–50.
St. Augustine of Hippo, "Sermon 48 on the New Testament." Revised and edited for New Advent by Kevin Knight, https://www.newadvent.org/fathers/160348.htm.

March 29: Wednesday of the Fifth Week of Lent
Richard Rohr, "The Truth Will Set You Free," June 14, 2020, Center for Action and Contemplation, https://cac.org/the-truth-will-set-you-free-2020-06-14/.

April 6: Holy Thursday
Pope Francis, Address to the Pilgrimage from El Salvador, October 30, 2015, https://www.vatican.va/content/francesco/en/speeches/2015/october/documents/papa-francesco_20151030_el-salvador.html.

April 7: Good Friday
Joan Chittister, "The Art of Silence," http://joanchittister.org/word-from-joan/art-silence.